Kintsukuroi

poems by

Whitnee Thorp

Finishing Line Press
Georgetown, Kentucky

Kintsukuroi

Copyright © 2017 by Whitnee Thorp
ISBN 978-1-63534-277-2 First Edition
All rights reserved under International and Pan-American Copyright Conventions.
No part of this book may be reproduced in any manner whatsoever without written permission from the publisher, except in the case of brief quotations embodied in critical articles and reviews.

ACKNOWLEDGMENTS

The following poems from the manuscript have been published in an earlier form:

"Typewriter" on *Splinter Generation* online 2012
"Here are my dying words" by *Emerge* Winter II 2013
"Coal Sweet" by *poemmemoirstory* 2014
"Eating Soup in China", "Silver Minnows", "A French teacher sets herself on fire", "Before Marriage", and "his name was samson" by *Pasque Petals* Fall 2015
"Sins Like Mine" in *Veils, Halos, Shackles* 2016
"& He Said" in *Poets Opposing Evil Trump* 2016
"Hands" in *Unprecedented Review* 2016
"Between Bus Stops in Zhangjiajie" forthcoming in *Jelly Bucket* 2017

Publisher: Leah Maines

Editor: Christen Kincaid

Cover Art: Andres Gallardo Jr

Author Photo: Doug Brewer

Cover Design: Elizabeth Maines McCleavy

Printed in the USA on acid-free paper.
Order online: www.finishinglinepress.com
also available on amazon.com

Author inquiries and mail orders:
Finishing Line Press
P. O. Box 1626
Georgetown, Kentucky 40324
U. S. A.

Table of Contents

Before Marriage 1
Drinking Tea 3
Eating Soup 4
Sins Like Mine 5
When a lie was made to feel like the truth 6
Sunflowers 7
Typewriter 8
A Girl 9
Between Bus Stops in Zhangjiajie 12
Silver Minnows 13
Carter, ... 14
Coming home from a deployment 17
Open 18
Saudade 19
Hands 22
My grandmother's brother is dying 23
Red 24
& He Said 25
his name was samson 26
A French teacher sets herself on fire 27
A Willow 28
Coal Sweet 29
Here are my dying words 30

To my mother & grandmother and their endless love.
To my family & countless friends who have supported me.
To my teachers & mentors who have taught me.

#NODAPL
Mni Wiconi

*Kintsukuroi- (n., Japanese) (v. phr.)- to repair with gold;
the art of repairing pottery with gold lacquer
with the understanding that the piece
is more beautiful for having been broken.*

Before Marriage

Mama's nails were painted red
and dishwater didn't make
her hands too rough to be held.
Her stomach was ironing board flat
and her lips pouted perfect
around half empty beer bottles.
When her face was summer freckled,
on the 4th of July, she swam naked in the river
before pressing his body
into the muddy bank of her own.

Before Mama,
Grandmama received letters
during the war from Billy
whose football kicks
couldn't save him
in the exploding marshes
across the black-eyed fish sea.
I've heard that for years afterward
she sprayed petunia perfume
and sealed those letters with lipstick kisses
that Billy would never receive,
before meeting Grandpa,
who only wore clip on ties
and only sold dictionaries door to door.

Before golden bands looped knuckles,
sepia prints of wedding-
cake-smeared faces,
and our first breaths
curled into the atmosphere.
Before hips widened with age,
coupons crowded wallets,
and our first baths.

Midnight stones were thrown
at closed windows,
car seats were laid flat,
and girls didn't wake
addled next to men

wondering if they had in fact
been the women who picked these sheets,
to match the comforter to the wallpaper,
and press the pillow shams.

Long before you were born
Mama wore a daisy in her hair
just behind her left ear
and no,
Daddy didn't give it to her.

Drinking Tea

My grandfather was
a Vietnam vet, the kind
that left with a rosary
around his neck and came back
with a right ring finger missing.

Some days while his tea cooled,
before the paper had been thrown
against the screen door, he'd look over
his pewter-rimmed glasses. Steam
curling to his wrinkled face,
fogging the lenses, just enough
where you could still see
his Southern Harebell blue eyes
behind them. His mouth curling
downwards at both ends and
his eyebrows molding
a riverbed of thought.

Did he feel the hot steam rising
from tropical fields, sweat sliding
down his uniform and bones cracking
beneath combat boot steps? The wet
marshes swallowing his legs?

Did he wade through smooth bamboo,
broken with his worn, tired body
or did he remember the slick
cool metal of his weapon
weighted on his heart?

Or was it the cry from the tea kettle,
shrill and long?
A yowling woman
in a hut-filled village,
her home burning
with her child left inside—
now the ash
in his teacup,
after the last sip.

Eating Soup in China

The foot of a chicken floats in my soup,
skin black like the charcoal
around a woman's eye when she wishes
to catch the sight of men
who need their feet—
or something else— washed
in night's dark creases.

Small spikes prick
my tongue, like the bent metal
of cola cans fished out of garbage pails
by bent-backed women,
with their hair white
and wild like tails of old monkeys.
They work beside
small-handed children,
cuts on their palms and barefoot,
topping trash-mountains.

But the chicken's claw
rolls around my tongue
like the words that clatter
among my tea-stained teeth,
words I hold back
when I hear of baby girls
pulled from their mothers,
pushed out like pulp
from sliced orange peels.

My words fight with the claw,
a feathered brawl against the silence,
then grab at my throat
as an old peasant man struck by a car is
left for dead on the dirt street.
His blood pools like Eastern sun
rising for the rooster's crow,
before the farmer picks up
his rice-fed chicken,
cracks the neck in one snap,
tosses the limp body into yellow dirt,
and readies the fire for morning soup.

Sins like Mine

I know the sins
of being touched
by my father
those nights when
my stomach
was as tight as my braids
beating around
on white pillows.
Sundays he sits
next to me in church,
cross in his hands,
Bible in my lap,
singing the Lord's praises
as I pray to Him
I will stop swelling.
Mama thinks
I'm just going to be tall
and tree-boned
like her own Mama was.
Scriptures taught
my sister and me
daily lessons about hell
burning unwashed sins,
but I cannot
bring myself to confess
that I have eyes
like mine
growing
inside.

When a lie was made to feel like the truth

I cracked my front tooth on a beer bottle,
fracturing it, like the
shelled   milky   skull
of the boy who died on the concrete in high school,
brain scrambled. He was left alone when thrown
through his windshield, pieces of glass
imbedded into his skin. But he deserved to die:
he was drinking and driving.

It happened the summer we moved to New York,
and I smoked the city in one setting. I inhaled the street-
bum love, rolling the crisp wet taste around my mouth
like a bladed apple from Halloween,
letting the pain   burn   my   lungs,
with exhaled taxi exhaust from the day you left
to accuse your mother
of sleeping with our elementary school gym teacher.
Little did you know,
the worms you released
would eat you as well,
eyes first.

Seeing images
of your mother's curled toes in stirrups,
a scalpel cutting petal-like membranes,
and the way she lay in bed for days
while your father made her eggs, and when he cracked
the shell and the yolk fell,
there were   tiny   spots   of   blood.

You remembered his eyes,
thick and wet
when he walked out of the kitchen,
leaving the eggs to burn out
the unknown specks
of life.

Sunflowers

Down next to the creek,
    where arrowheads sink
    in the yellow-mud banks,
    waiting to be found
    and saved in pockets,

Behind the old corner store,
    where a checkers game always half-played
    rests on the glass counter
    and Monday morning gossip scatters
    like white-tipped dandelion heads,

Next to Miss May's burned
    down home, where only a front porch
    survived and neighborhood cats
    sleep in the day, caterwaul
    during fights, losing tails and eyes—

my home.

It smells of tall-stemmed sunflowers
    always watching, with hundreds
    of black-speckled eyes. Waiting each day
    for their sight to be plucked by the blackbird,
        hoping they will outgrow his reach.

When I am outside alone,
    Mama's frying pork chops
    and Daddy's out deep in the fields,
    I try to grab what is really there,
    grow myself to the sun.

The slap of a wet washrag
    on Mama's thigh that snaps me back
    to chores waiting to be done.

Years ago those old blackbirds
plucked her eyes.

Typewriter

On Sundays
my grandmother and I
would visit her ex-husband,
my grandfather, at his apartment
a block away from ours. On Sundays,
the typewriter would be in the same spot,
at the head of the table
covering a yellow smoke-stained place mat.
He'd roll a papyrus-thin white paper
through the typewriter's rounded black tongue.
His heavy fingers, made for a military gun,
rolled the paper to just the right spot.
I'd then single-fingerly samba across its lettered teeth,
as my grandparents sat across the table from each other
and talked about nothing. My grandmother would hold
her coffee cup close to her lips,
cooling it with her sighs like the hiss of a faint teapot.
My grandfather ashed at the end
of spoken thoughts, scattering bits of his life
onto the laminated wood tabletop.

On Sundays
I wake next to men
with thin comb-overs and
tattoos on their forearms,
faded colors and lines
of posed women or lion heads.
They offer coffee like he did,

and their walls, once white,
are a pale yellow with a tinge of brown
around the creases from all the smoke,
from all the years. In the middle of their kitchen
tables sit bowls of hard ruby wrapped candies,
with a few spare lighters poking out.
While they saunter around their apartments
in terry cloth robes and ten-year-old slippers,
I often search their bedroom closets for a typewriter—
one I never find.

A Girl

Sharing the same bed with you
for almost a year,

was something neither of us
could pinpoint why we kept doing it.

Why we found ourselves
beneath sheets not made on Saturdays,

bodies entangled in darkness
until the next day spread her lips
shuffling us back to reality.

      It was not a relationship.

Yet I remember the night
your eyes floated with guilt,

as you told me, you had slept with someone
else during the time of us.

Guilty too—I lied,
a lower number crept out.

After that it was 4 am & we ate
salami on toasted, buttered bread

in silence, in your kitchen,
that always had crumbs
sprinkled across the floor.

Weeks later in the same kitchen,
you asked if I wanted to take a summer trip

to South Carolina.
& I immediately said,

I didn't meet parents.
& we laughed.

& I remembered months before

crouched naked in your bed
over your worn high school yearbooks

you told me the highlight reels
of your mind

all the football games, plays, & moves
engraved in your memory.

After you had said, *the girl
I take home,
I'll marry.*

Now there are less than 30 days before you marry
the girl, we both knew back in college.

A bird-like blonde, always smiling & nodding
& believing whoever she could.

        She is everything I am not.

I see photos on social media,
you hugging your baby

you had with her. His sweet nose,
& rolls on elbows & knees.

Will he ever know of
a dad who once slow danced

in his college bedroom,
cheek pressed to her hairline,

hands intertwined like lace,
swaying soft, to his hummed song

& only a bedside lamp on, glowing
around two bodies on fire,

extinguished only by each other?

Will he ever know of a girl, not his mother?

Between Bus Stops in Zhangjiajie

I push Ipod earbuds
deep into my head,

dropping my Yuan into
the box that eats bus fares.

The driver grunts, smiles
a brown toothed grin.

The floor is spit-slick,
peppered with drips of sweat

from farmers standing like scarecrows;
on horizontal bars across their shoulders,

they balance baskets
of barley and black tea.

Babies, swaddled in dirty
Mickey Mouse printed

blankets, suck on chopped
sugar cane.

My bus seat rattles
the way a plane would

right before a crash,
before the sudden drop,

heart crawling to your tongue.
Before you can think

about how you ignored
your Mother's last call

or how sometimes
you still think about the one

who woke early, disappearing
quickly as bodies do.

Silver Minnows

The spider-shaped pond
had deep mud
around its spindle legs.
The water, the color
of dried blood.

We waded in the belly
where minnows swam,
their pouted lips
grazing our knob-knees.
When we stood very still
you'd reach down
and snatch one.
Little tail wiggling out
the backdoor of your fist.

Once, when you lost
your front tooth, I dared
you to eat one. You dangled
the minnow above your lips, letting it slip
where your tooth once was.

The spider pond is now
cracked earth, speckled
with seeds dropped by passing birds.

When I think of you,
I picture that glimmering body slipping
into that black hole,
a place where it never should have been.

Carter,

When you are lowered
into Kentucky's
December-yellow mud
during the 21 gun salute,
will you promise to return?

Like the specks and grains
on a gardener's hands,
rimming nail beds after
she sows seeds of life
to grow Kentucky thick
with vein-eared tobacco leaves?

Or will you be fallen
dust on the velvet stems
of smooth-skinned tomatoes?

Will you settle
at the bottom of a creek bed,
or on the end of a lure,
tangled in the neon membranes
which ripple over rocks glossed
with teal moss, right before the creek
is swallowed up by the large-mouthed river?

Or will you linger
on the slippery spotted lips
of a smallmouth, one that you threw back
with your grandson, two summers ago?

Will you emboss yourself into
the fine print, finding your name
in the last letter of a brown leather
bound Bible? Will you be buried
among the gold flecks of a faith
you praised daily, guiding
others to find the Holy Spirit
every time the spine is cracked?

Or will you, when dew still beads
on magnolia leaves, reside in the spaces
between an organ's keys, in a church
during an early Sunday morning service?
Will you quiver between vibrations
of soft sung hymns?

Will you return
in gentle-breathed wind,
which flies stripes above troops
stationed in deserts,
who look up at
the crow-eye black skies,
those that crack with rockets
and the glimmer of stars?

Will you be their peace—
the same illumination
their families see,
when they look up, simply
missing moments, where they
don't have to say anything,
but know the other person
is near?

Will you be our moments
of silence when people
give condolences,
when we still feel your warmth
around our shoulders?

Or maybe you will ride out
on the floating spots we see
after closing our eyes too long
when we sink
into life without you?

Could you please find time
to visit between the changing

of traffic lights, when we find
ourselves alone again,
driving familiar routes?

Or can you tuck yourself
into the chuckle before it
hums from our lips, erupting
into our first laugh
without you?

While you become all,
always return
in those moments
when the blue life
in your eyes grows faint,
or your sillage fades
from hanging sweaters.

Please Carter,
return on the grace
of each of our given days,
and settle into the closing
of our lips when we say,

Amen.

Coming together after a deployment

the joining of two,
who once knew the inside crevices
of one another's bodies and thoughts,
the moles never checked by doctors,
the scars never healed,
the flesh never kissed by mothers.

—Yet together after a deployment,
is the unplanned shuffle in a grocery aisle.
A stranger reaching for sugar, smiling
and you cart-curving to fit,
while list-checking, and thinking
what comes next.

There's a moment
when bodies seem familiar,
until nights crack open engulfed
in night time terrors.
You can do nothing
but wake to the jolting tremors
of body muscles flinching,
and tensing from what
you can not see.
You can touch lightly and coo,
*It's alright. Wake up. You're here
in our apartment now.*

You can
take a heavy head and
lay it on your shoulder's scoop,
stroking temple lines, rippling away dreams
of a reality that was only 3 weeks ago.
You can only slide your foot next to theirs
beneath the cool side of the sheets,
and rub your sole
on the top of their veined-leaf foot;
a reminder your bodies are alive
and survived.

Open

Give me
        your wide
                mouth,
offing-like
        and deep.
             An ocean
visible
        from land.

Saudade

> "The Portuguese call it saudade: a longing for something so indefinite as to be indefinable. Love affairs, miseries of life, the way things were, people already dead, those who left and the ocean that tossed them on the shores of a different land—all things born of the soul that can only be felt."—Anthony De Sa

I.

My Aunt Brenda
was my mother's first friend,
after we moved to
Kentucky, leaving
my father to drink.

Together they worked as maids,
shuffling carts filled with
small bottled shampoos,
toothbrushes never used,
and dirty towels.

II.

There was always a smile
stretched wide across
my Aunt Brenda's
smooth coffee-skinned face.
Before she would crack
a deep-rooted laugh,
she would say, "Aw—"
showing a small gold heart
planted on her front tooth,
glimmering.

Her nails were always filed
into a slight square, corners rounded.
And she would let me,
a constant-nervous nail biter,
trace the polished edges
with my small child-fingers.

Every day she wore
a brown leather-banded Garfield watch,
his striped tail ticking the time,
and when the University of Kentucky
basketball team played
she would bring Big Macs, fries,
and let me sip her Coke
during commercial breaks.

She taught me, when my curly
unruly hair was pulled up tight,
to peck it, instead of scratching
if I had an itch, so as not to release
strands of kink. And before
I went to 4H camp, she came over,
corn-rowing my long coiling
locks, and I loved them
because they matched
her silky braids.

III.

Years later,
in her hospital room,
I held her fragile veined hands
and outlined her nails
with my pointer finger.
I rubbed her dry straw-like
hair, tracing to her temples.
Traced her frail collar bone,
finding the nook where God
had pressed His thumb too hard.

She lay quiet, too tired to visit.
But did not want me to leave.

Her Garfield watch
had been stolen
from her beside table
when they took her

for another MRI,
for another diagnosis,
for more bad news,

that the cancer
had spread further
in her delicate body.

IV.

In those moments of longing,
what was uncurling our spirits
from the love that remains,
from what can only be felt,
was all we had time for.

Hands

        I pray into the early light,
        entranced with my own, smooth hands,

        that have not built the life
        I had imagined.

My Mama's hands
were rough from shucking corn,

snapping green string beans,
and soaking in cloudy dishwater.

Her hands, wide and callused,
propped my brother and me

on her broad hips
when we were too tired to walk,

yanked us from climbed trees,
or smacked our legs when we tattled.

At Bible study, she
clapped to the rhythm of the Holy Ghost,

and squeezed Daddy's thick knuckles
during quiet prayers, breathy hymns.

Once, when I had a fever, late at night,
she rubbed bits of ice on my dirty-child feet.

I've tried to reimagine every night
before sleep envelopes me and the next day is conscious

those hands
when they made clover necklaces for grandbabies,

pulled lambs from wet wombs,
rubbed the swollen fingers of dying parents,

and sewed mismatched buttons
onto plaid work shirts.

My grandmother's brother is dying

and his wife ignores calls.
The hospital phone chirrups

every few minutes as his wife
paces next to the window, its curtains pulled.

His eyes are open but he is blind.
Church folk gather

clucking gossip as they pick
Kentucky Fried Chicken legs

down to the bone, while his bones
ache down to the marrow. Tubes run

narrow paths and are covered
when his other sisters visit.

They rub his swollen purple hands.
His black curls are matted against

two pillows pressed crisp, like his Army uniform
when he was a younger, fighting man.

When he took women with one hand
by their waists, spun them around

until their skirts were blossoming brugmansias.
In those days a wink and a whisper

unbuttoned blouses
on beds made by maids.

Now he lies with
the Bible open on his lap,

its pages worn and gold-rimmed.
His eyes are glass, delicate
and clear to the other side.

Red

Yesterday, I woke
to blood, thick
and clotted
on my thighs.
Mama smiled.
I cried.

& He Said

> "All of the men, we're petrified to speak to women anymore. We may raise our voice. You know what? The women get it better than we do, folks. They get it better than we do."—Donald Trump

If by better do you mean,
for every dollar earned by a man
a woman, with the same
education & background
will only hear 79 cents
clink in the bottom of her purse?
Or 59 cents if she is Native American or 60
cents if she is African American?
Or the woman with a graduate degree
will not be able to provide
like the man with a bachelor's degree?

If by better do you mean,
single mothers, women of color,
& elderly women
are at the highest risk
of going to bed without dinner, eviction
from broken-fenced homes, &
will be known in this century
as the invisible poor?

If by better do you mean,
when 1 in 5 women will be raped
no matter their clothes,
drinks consumed, or if they are
walking home because the majority
will be raped by men
who they know & trust most?

Mr. Trump,
the war on women
has long been waged
but we can say
your rhetoric & forked tongue-talk
will not be the apple
we choose to bite today.

his name was samson

and his beard grew long,
hair too, tangled dark
until i combed
it with long strokes,
holding brown knots
between my palms,
sitting cross-legged on our bed
behind the broadness of his shoulders.

as i braided his hair tight,
he'd shut his eyes,
chin to chest,
whispering a prayer
for us
while i'd kiss his neck, lightly,
and trace my nails down
the wine-red scar on his right arm,
left from a lion's grip,
until the candle went out
and we were left to love in the darkness.

one night the jawbone
went missing from our bedside
while he slept and all was still
until the morning's yellow light
lit the sheared locks of hair
on his white pillow.

i pressed the brown braid
between my praying palms,
whispering
for us.

in the distance pillars fall,
crushing a blind man's bones.

A French teacher sets herself on fire

in the playground. Petrol drips
onto hopscotch chalk.
The match, slow to burn, ignites quick,
savoring the taste of her burning flesh.

She is a quiet woman
even as the flames wolf her down,
the fire a starving dog given meat.
Her mouth is opened,
but the heat has already
singed her screams.

While attending the University,
when asked why she wanted
to teach, she said,
"Because my heart burns
to kindle the joy of learning in others."

Never thinking her body would
dance a smoke-scarfed tango
beneath the yellow-turned sky.
Her hot skin melts
to candle wax, her arms outstretch
to grab God's gowns
before the Devil rips through the earth
and seizes her feet. Her spine cracks
and pops from the heat like the pages
of old love letters thrown into the fire,
burning from the outside in.

A Willow

Sylvia was a willow branch,
at 17. Her sunken cheeks matched
her deep-running roots, like her
grandmother had. She was long and thin,
with pliant hips widened from giving birth
at such a young age. She was unwed
with a daughter from a married man,
who would not leave his pursed-lipped wife
or their bed-bound child, who had wisps for legs.

Weeks after giving birth, in her childhood bed,
Sylvia's strong shoulders carried water
deep into the black dusted Magoffin County
coal mines. She followed the sweet songs
of little black-eyed canaries singing and found
light from thirsty miners, black-soot dipped men—
who only had the whites of eyes left.

Then, she was called for.
A Nichols man, tall with
Basswood-brown skin, who came
from Ohio and he needed a wife.
His had burned up in their home,
and he was left with four children,
who needed a mother.

At 18, Sylvia's willow branches bent
and her roots settled in new ground,
as she kissed the sweaty foreheads of children
before they said their prayers.

Coal Sweet

my mama
recalls stories
of her father
whose lungs were black

as the coal that weighed
down his coffin
on the day he died
in july

a man who drank
milk with blackberries
packed his pipe
with a nail-less thumb

and she can't remember
shedding a tear
or what hymn
he'd hum in the truck

or which flannel
was his Sunday-best
but does
remember

it was the day
she tasted
cinnamon
for the first time

Here are my dying words

the ones that never slipped
from my lips,
but chiseled their way
through the marrow
of my pen, to a notebook
shut in a forgotten drawer:

Please,
remember me as I was,
not as I am. Round face, curly hairline,
cross-legged on a barstool. The nights
when laughter stretched my face
to something unrecognizable,
or when I'd hold a baby,
counting its toes
and bite my lip.

Don't speak of me
as always good, because I wasn't—
no one can be.
I am, or was,
layered mistakes, what ifs,
jumbled-around bed sheets,
missed flights, unanswered texts,
dates lied to for the hope of something better,
or the ease of something familiar—
something pushed into a pocket, saved.

When you speak of how my breaths
spiraled into space,
don't treat me like a fragile figurine
in your grandmother's dining room cabinet.
But as one whose heartbeat you heard
thumping, ear pressed to my chest
on New Year's Eve. Confetti nesting
on your lashes, neon lights bouncing
over watch faces, reflections
of bodies dancing in plastic crowns,
floating colors—
living.

Whitnee Thorp is from Lexington, KY but currently lives in Box Elder, SD, where she teaches on the Pine Ridge Indian Reservation at Oglala Lakota College. She has her MFA in Creative Writing from the Bluegrass Writers Studio at Eastern Kentucky University. Some of her publications include *PMS Poemmemoirstory*, *Veils, Halos, and Shackles*, *Pasque Petals*, *Poets Opposing Evil Trump*, and Tom Hunley's *Poetry Gymnasium*.

She has attended the Disquiet International Writing Residency in Lisbon, Portugal, Wellstone Writing Residency, KY Governor's School for the Arts, among other writing conferences and workshops. She recently won the South Dakota Poetry Society's annual chapbook contest with her chapbook, *Cicurate*.

When Whitnee isn't writing, you can find her binge watching Netflix shows, drinking a Mountain Dew, or eating some Hot Cheetos.

www.ingramcontent.com/pod-product-compliance
Lightning Source LLC
LaVergne TN
LVHW041602070426
835507LV00011B/1247